This
Nature Storybook
belongs to:

....

....

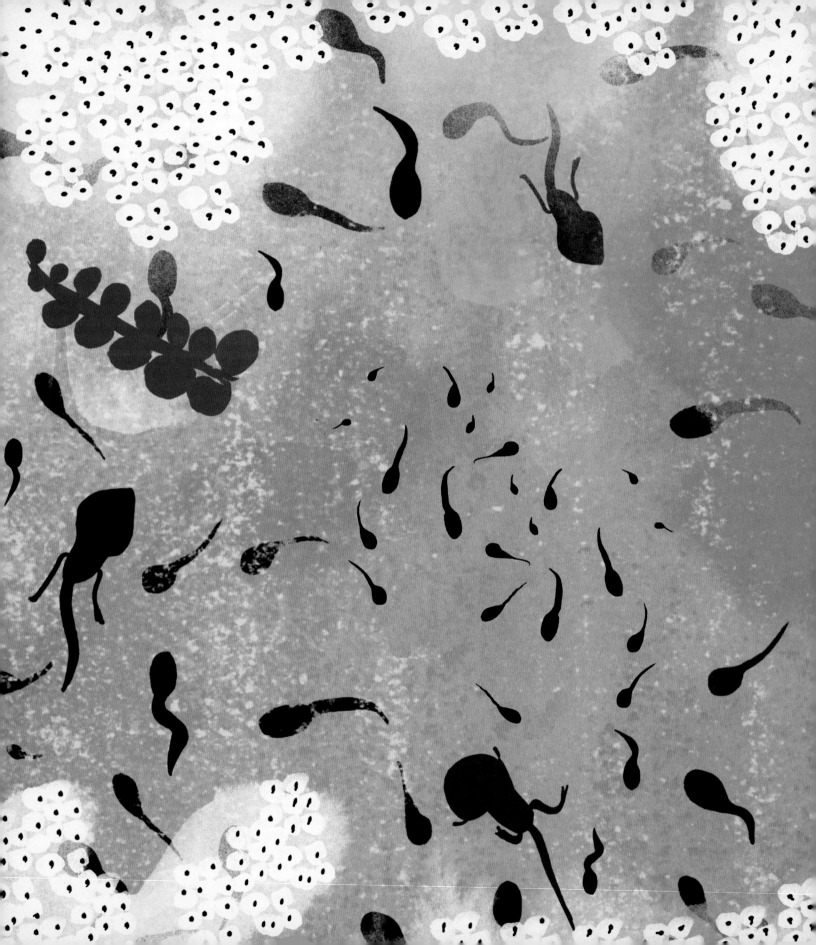

Did you know that there are more than 5,000 different kinds of frog altogether? Each one is different but they have some things in common.

Frogs all have short bodies, big back legs, smaller front legs and no tail. Almost all of them can jump, but some can only manage short hops. They eat small animals like snails, slugs, worms, beetles and flies.

Frogs do some of their breathing through their skin, and usually live in damp places. Most kinds are found in warm parts of the world where it rains a lot. The ones that live where the winter is chilly, like a lot of North America and Europe, hibernate and come out in spring to breed.

Nearly all frogs lay eggs – usually in water, in a pond or a stream – that hatch out into tadpoles with a tail but no legs. They don't look anything like their parents.

As a tadpole grows older, its tail begins to shrink and it starts to sprout back and front legs.

Eventually the tail disappears and the tadpole becomes a tiny frog.

Fabulous

Martin Jenkins

For
my family
M.J.

For
Richard & Adrian
T.H.

WALKER BOOKS
AND SUBSIDIARIES
LONDON · BOSTON · SYDNEY · AUCKLAND

First published 2015 by Walker Books Ltd, 87 Vauxhall Walk, London SE11 5HJ   This edition published 2016   10 9 8 7 6 5 4 3 2 1   Text © 2015 Martin Jenkins   Illustrations © 2015 Tim Hopgood   The right of Martin Jenkins and Tim Hopgood to be identified as author and illustrator respectively of this work has been asserted by them in accordance with the Copyright, Designs and Patents Act 1988   This book has been typeset in Avenir and Imperfect   Printed in China   All rights reserved. No part of this book may be reproduced, transmitted or stored in an information retrieval system in any form or by any means, graphic, electronic or mechanical, including photocopying, taping and recording, without prior written permission from the publisher.   British Library Cataloguing in Publication Data: a catalogue record for this book is available from the British Library   ISBN 978-1-4063-6599-3   www.walker.co.uk

FSC
www.fsc.org
MIX
Paper from
responsible sources
FSC® C101537

Frogs

illustrated by

Tim Hopgood

This frog is **huge**

(for a frog).

It's a Goliath Frog and it lives
in West Africa. It's the biggest
frog in the world. Sometimes
it eats other frogs!

These ones are tiny.

This is the smallest kind of frog in the world, or at least the smallest that anybody knows about.
It lives in New Guinea.

And this one has got a very odd nose.

It's called Darwin's Frog and
it lives in South America. No one
really knows why it's got a pointy nose.

oops …

This frog can …

... jump really far,
really quickly.

It's a Striped Rocket Frog from Australia and
it can jump five metres in one go: very handy
for escaping from enemies in a hurry.

croak

ribbit

honk

rack-rack

And these ones make an awful lot of noise.

churp

Frogs call to let other frogs know they are there. All these are male frogs. Female frogs are much quieter. The big one in the middle is a bullfrog.

15

This one is called
a Flying Frog,
although it can't
really fly.

It lives in trees in forests in Southeast Asia.
It spreads out the skin between its toes to help it
float in the air when it jumps from tree to tree.

And this one is called a Hairy Frog, although it doesn't have any proper hairs.

The Hairy Frog lives in West Africa. The things that look like hairs are little strips of skin. They probably help the frog breathe when it's underwater.

I think these frogs
are all very beautiful.

I couldn't tell you which one
was the MOST
beautiful.

But I can tell you that each one could kill a horse, though only if the horse was silly enough to try to eat it.

A horse wouldn't eat a frog on purpose, but plenty of other animals might. South American Arrow Poison Frogs have deadly poison in their skins to help protect them. Their bright colours are a way of saying **KEEP AWAY!**

19

These frogs make
a nest of foam for their eggs.

20 They're African Grey Tree Frogs. Their nests hang in branches over a pond or stream.
When the eggs in the nests hatch, the tadpoles wriggle out and drop into the water below.

And the one with the very odd nose looks after its babies in its throat!

The male Darwin's Frog snaps up the eggs just before they hatch and keeps the tadpoles in a special pouch in his throat. You'd think he would swallow them down by accident, but he never seems to.

This frog never leaves the water.

It's an African Clawed Frog.
It spends its whole life living in a stream
or pond. Not many frogs do that.

And this frog can live buried in the ground for years and years …

waiting …

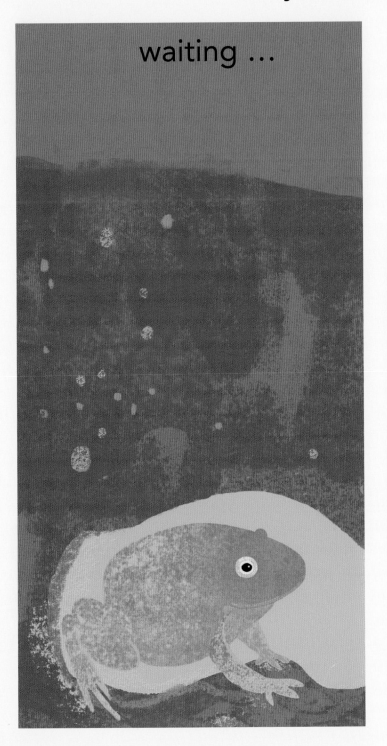

for the rain.

It's an Australian Water-holding Frog and it lives in the desert. It makes a little room for itself where it stays cool and damp. When it rains and the ground gets wet, the frog digs itself out.

All

these frogs are wonderful, but ...

25

... my favourite frog of all is the medium-sized, greeny-brown one that sits on a lily pad in my back garden pond!

Martin Jenkins has come across a lot of different kinds of frog in his work as a conservation biologist. He thinks they're all wonderful, even the ones that have sometimes kept him awake at night. **Tim Hopgood** was fascinated by frogspawn when he was little and has enjoyed the chance to draw some actual frogs now that he's big. Both of them wanted to get as many frogs as possible into this book, so here are a few more, just for fun.

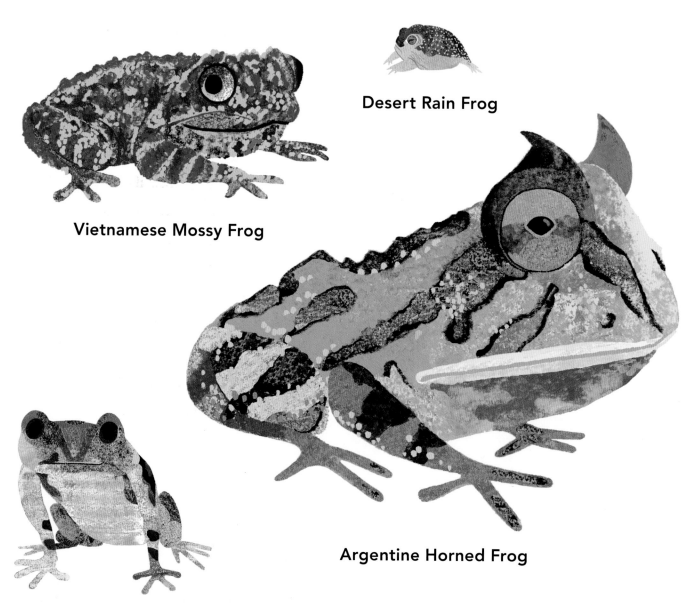

Desert Rain Frog

Vietnamese Mossy Frog

Argentine Horned Frog

Malagasy Rainbow Frog

Painted Reed Frog

Whitebelly Reed Frog

Splendid Leaf Frog

Black Rain Frog

Index

Look up the pages to find out about all these froggy things. Don't forget to look up both kinds of word **this kind** – and this kind.

breathe 17

digs 23

eats 9, 19

eggs 20–21

huge 8–9

jumps 14, 16

noise 15

nose 12, 21

poison 19

pond 20, 22, 27

tadpoles 20–21

throat 21

tiny 10–11

MORE INFORMATION
Martin Jenkins says the best place to find out about frogs is **amphibiaweb.org**. You can also find a lot of useful information at **iucnredlist.org** and **arkive.org** and on Wikipedia.

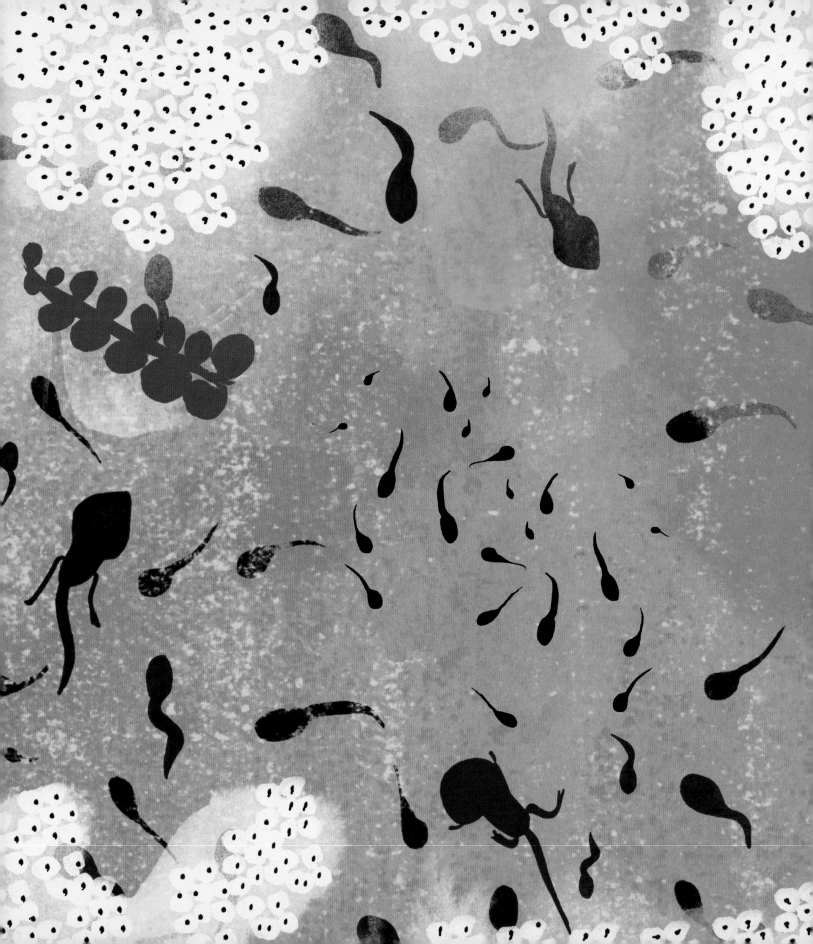

Note to Parents

Sharing books with children is one of the best ways to help them learn. And it's one of the best ways they learn to read, too.

Nature Storybooks are beautifully illustrated, award-winning information picture books whose focus on animals has a strong appeal for children. They can be read as stories, revisited and enjoyed again and again, inviting children to become excited about a subject, to think and discover, and to want to find out more.

Each book is an adventure into the real world that broadens children's experience and develops their curiosity and understanding – and that's the best kind of learning there is.

Note to Teachers

Nature Storybooks provide memorable reading experiences for children in Key Stages 1 and 2 (Years 1–4), and also offer many learning opportunities for exploring a topic through words and pictures.

By working with the stories, either individually or together, children can respond to the animal world through a variety of activities, including drawing and painting, role play, talking and writing.

The books provide a rich starting-point for further research and for developing children's knowledge of information genres.

Nature Storybooks support the literacy curriculum in a variety of ways, providing:

- a focus for a whole class topic
- high-quality texts for guided reading
- a resource for the class read-aloud programme
- information texts for the class and school library for developing children's individual reading interests

Find more information on how to use Nature Storybooks in the classroom at
www.walker.co.uk/naturestorybooks
Nature Storybooks support KS 1–2 English and KS 1–2 Science